Hohokam
Arts and Crafts

Written by **Barbara Gronemann**
Designed by **Lisa Bohman**

Southwest Learning Sources, Inc.
6440 E. Presidio Road
Scottsdale, Arizona 85254-3970
(480) 991-0341
bgronemann@aol.com

Acknowledgments

Sincere thanks go to the following:

Arizona archaeologists who reviewed this publication, Jerry Howard, Curator of Anthropology, Mesa Southwest Museum, and Ann Valdo Howard, Archaeology Public Programs Director/ Archaeologist, State Historic Preservation Office.

Arizona Teachers who reviewed this publication, Donna Benge, Ida Redbird School, Mesa; Judy Given, Kachina School, Peoria; Pat Dowd, former President of Arizona Art Education Association and former Arts in Education Coordinator for the Phoenix Arts Commission; and the many friends who reviewed and made helpful comments.

Copy editing by Linda Gregonis, Editor / Indexer, Archaeologist.

Credits:

Pueblo Grande Museum - Shell Etching Activity
ESAA Cultural Arts - Sandpaper Petroglyph Activity

First Edition printed in the United States
Second Printing 1997
Third Printing 2009

Library of Congress Catalog Card Number: 93-87184
ISBN 0-9657406-0-9

Dedication

**To my family who support
my interests in the Southwest.**

Contents

	page
Preface	v
The Hohokam	1
Hohokam Ceramics	3
Coiling a Small Pot	5
Slipping and Polishing a Small Pot	6
Clay Figurines	7
Hohokam Shell Jewelry	8
Etching Shell	10
Shell Bead Necklace	11
Mosaic Shell Pendant	12
Hohokam Cotton Spinning	13
Spindles	15
Spinning with Cotton	16
Dyeing Cotton Yarn	17
Hohokam Cloth Weaving	18
Warping a Loom	20
Plain Weaving	21
Removing the Weaving	22
Hohokam Basket Weaving	23
Plaiting a Mat	25
Coiling a Basket	26
Hohokam Gourds	27
A Bag Rattle	29
Gourd Ring Toss Game	30
Hohokam Rock Art	31
Creating a Petroglyph	33
Hohokam Designs	37
References	45

Preface

Hohokam Arts And Crafts fell into a natural format as I compiled the many lessons and ideas that I have presented to children and adults as former Museum Educator at the Pueblo Grande Museum and as Educator and Research Specialist in my own business, Southwest Learning Sources. It is my wish to pass on these activities so that all ages can have a "hands-on" experience with the arts and crafts of the Hohokam. When I told my daughter about this en-deavor, she was excited to help. She was perfect for the job since she has a degree in graphic design from the University of Arizona.

Crafts covered in this publication are not all that the Hohokam accomplished. It is my hope to include others in future editions.

Each section presents a Hohokam craft, beginning with archaeological and ethnohistorical background information. It is as accurate as possible according to what has been learned to date by archaeologists in their excavations of Hohokam sites. The drawings on these pages are of Hohokam artifacts, with the exceptions of the drawings of the Pima loom, gourd ring game, and burden basket.

The border used throughout the book is a portion of the Hohokam pottery design on the cover. A page of borders along with six pages of Hohokam design elements are included in the back of the book for those who wish to be authentic in their Hohokam creations. These were used artistically by the Hohokam on their craft forms.

The reference pages list books used for the research on the Hohokam along with books of interest for further reading.

To correct any errors in my research, this book has been edited by archaeologists who are Hohokam experts and teachers who present archaeology in the classroom.

Every age can enjoy this book and have many hours of fun exploring the arts and crafts of the Hohokam. I hope that each activity tried in the book will lead to a better understanding of and appreciation for these prehistoric people who found time to put aesthetics into everyday creations.

The Hohokam

The Hohokam lived in the Sonoran Desert in central and southern Arizona from approximately 200 - 1450 CE. The heartland of the Hohokam is often thought of as in the vicinity of modern Phoenix along the Salt and Gila Rivers. Although some details about Hohokam origins are uncertain, there is a consensus among archaeologists that the Hohokam culture developed out of the local hunting and gathering group referred to as the "Late Southwestern Archaic" sometime after the time of Christ.

The name Hohokam is from the Upper Piman language of the Pima people who call themselves Akimel O'odahm, or River People. The English translation of Hohokam varies with context: all used up, consumed, perished, deceased, all gone.

As the Archaic hunting and gathering groups (who preceded the Hohokam) gradually increased their reliance on domesticated plants, they began to build more substantial dwellings and semi-permanent communities evolved. This phase of transition is known as the Red Mountain phase (100 - 200 CE). It is thought by some field archaeologist that it was during this phase that the Hohokam culture developed out of the "Late Southwestern Archaic". This area of the Hohokam history is still not clear.

Some archaeologist think that the people were farming in Arizona and relying primarily on farming for their subsistence some time after 1 CE. Their gardens were planted with maize (corn), beans, squash, cotton, and agave. There is some evidence that they also domesticated barley as well as cholla, agave and amaranth. They engineered large, long canals to divert water from the rivers for the irrigation of their crops. They built some of the largest and most sophisticated irrigation systems ever constructed without machinery. Over 500 miles of their canals have thus far been recorded. Their agricultural economy developed not only along the banks of the Salt and the Gila rivers, but along the New River, Tonto Creek, San Pedro, Agua Fria, Verde, and Santa Cruz rivers as well.

The Hohokam constructed semisubterranean houses, called "pithouses" by archaeologists. The floors of these houses were dug into the ground. They were plastered with a mixture of caliche and clay. There were large posts for the main roof supports with smaller supports outlining the houses. The frameworks were covered with plant materials and then sometimes topped with mud. Above-ground adobe rooms appeared later in the Hohokam occupation, around 1200 CE.

Some of the Hohokam villages had ballcourts and platform mounds. The ballcourts could have been used for a ball game similar to that played in Mexico or for other ritualistic or ceremonial purposes. Platform mounds eventually replaced the ballcourts as major public facilities. These massive earthen mounds had house-like structures on top and might have been temples.

The Hohokam became highly skilled craftspeople and traded their wares throughout the Southwest. Their work in carved stone and shell is exceptional. Their shell jewelry was an important trade item. They etched, painted, carved shell, and manufactured fine shell bracelets from whole shells. Necklaces were strung with whole shell and cut disc beads. They made earrings, rings, and pendants. They also crafted mosaic overlay, gluing small rectangular pieces of turquoise onto shells carved into frog or bird designs.

The Hohokam made a distinctive red-on-buff and red ware pottery using the paddle and anvil technique. They slipped their red ware pottery and gave it a fine sheen by using a polishing stone.

They used stones to peck designs on the boulders in their environment. These pecked elements are known as petroglyphs. Some of their designs were painted with mineral paints. These are called pictographs. Their designs are either abstract or representational in style. Sometimes the elements make up a planned composition. Life forms depicted include human figures, big horn sheep, deer, dogs, turtles, lizards, snakes, birds, and insects. Geometric designs and mazes were also important. There are circle designs everywhere. The hallmark of Hohokam rock art is the spiral.

The Hohokam tradition ended sometime after 1450 CE. The collapse of the Hohokam is poorly understood and difficult to explain and is still a major question being examined by scholars today.

Sonoran Desert - Boundaries vary when defined according to climate, rainfall, flora or vegetation. In general, the Sonoran Desert lies in most of the SW of Arizona, the SE corner of California, the NW of the state of Sonora, Mexico, and most of Baja California, Mexico.

Hohokam - The Akimel O'odham (Pima) word meaning "all used up," "consumed," or "all gone".

Domestication - Making something suitable for human use such as taming wild animals or farming wild plants.

Archaeologist - The scientist who studies the people who lived in the past by analysis of the materials they left behind.

Pithouse - A house with a floor and part of the walls dug into the ground. The walls extending above ground were made with sticks, grasses, and mud.

Caliche - Crusted calcium carbonate formed on certain soils in dry regions by evaporation of rising solutions.

Hohokam Ceramics

It is thought by some archaeologists that pottery making came into the American Southwest from northern Mexico. The earliest pottery found in the Hohokam culture dates to around 200 CE. Through excavations and analyses of pot sherds (pottery pieces) and whole vessels, archaeologists have learned the sequence of Hohokam pottery development, types of clays, tempers, slips, and paints used, as well as manufacturing and firing techniques.

The Hohokam probably gathered their clay from dug out pits, the canals, river beds, or the bases of mountains as potters do today. Elongated pits lined with clay were their mixing basins. Their buff or brown clay was tempered with crushed stone such as micaceous schist, quartz, feldspar, and sand to keep the pot from cracking when heated with a wood fire to harden it. They used a coiling technique for building their pottery walls. The clay was rolled into rope-like lengths and wrapped or coiled around a clay base. This is the coiling technique. A paddle and anvil was then used to smooth the coiled walls. The paddle was of wood and looked like a spatula. It was used to beat the coils on the exterior of the vessel, bonding and thinning them and at the same time shaping the walls. The anvil was a smooth rounded stone or mushroom shape made from clay or stone that was held by the stem. It was the supporting tool and was placed on the interior of the vessel while the paddle beat at the exterior wall.

Clay vessels for cooking, serving, and storage were most commonly made by the Hohokam, but ladles, scoops, figurines, spindle whorls, and vessels in the shapes of animals or people (effigy vessels) were also manufactured. One distinctive vessel shape has become a hallmark of the Hohokam pottery. It has a short, necked mouth and instead of a smooth and rounded wall, a ridge like a shoulder juts out low on the body of the vessel. This is called a Gila shoulder.

After a pot was completed, it may have been coated with a slip (thinned clay usually of a different color), painted with a design, or just left plain. The Hohokam also incised patterns in the soft clay, using a pointed stick as a tool. Sometime the moist slip would be polished by rubbing a smooth stone back and forth upon it.

The Hohokam also painted their clay vessels with red designs. Their designs were painted with an iron oxide paint (a red earth containing iron oxide minerals) with brushes made from yucca leaves or grass stems. Small geometric or life forms, both human and animal, were painted in a rhythmic repetitive pattern on their pottery. They used lines extensively as a design element. Broad lines, fringed lines, lines of hatching, wavy lines of hatching, cross-hatching, and interlocking scrolls.

Large pits have been uncovered by archaeologists where Hohokam fired or baked their pottery in an open fire of wood. The Hohokam sometimes purposely blackened the insides of their bowls by a technique called smudging. Smoldering materials placed inside of bowls during firing, let off sooty smoke, causing the inside of the vessel to blacken when the carbon particles penetrated the pores of the pot. Sometimes the inside of the bowl was polished before the firing so that the finished vessel was a polished, smudged ware.

Sherd - A piece or fragment of a broken pot.

Effigy - Images of animals or people carved of stone or formed of clay, sometimes a part of a container.

Incise - To cut or engrave into, such as soft clay with a stick.

Hatching - A set of lines made parallel to each other.

Smudging - The blackening of the inside of a bowl by placing a smoldering fire in it when it is baked.

Coiling a Small Pot

Materials

***AARDVAK®* gray clay cone .06 -** It is not necessary to knead this clay. (Other types of clay may also be used.)
Masking tape - Tape the wax paper square to a flat surface. Run the tape completely across the top and the bottom of the square.
Sandwich bag - Place an 8 oz. piece of clay in the bag. Close the bag after each removal of clay.

Wooden spoon - 3 5/8" craft size
Small bowl - cover just the bottom with water
Smooth rounded stone - or halves of plastic eggs
Corrugated cardboard - cut a 5" by 7" square
Wax paper - cut a 12" by 14" square
Toothpicks

This pot may be taken to a ceramic shop and fired in a kiln at cone .06. Allow it to dry about a week before firing.

1. Shape and roll a small amount of clay into a ball about 2" in diameter.

2. Flatten the ball of clay between the fingers forming a round patty about 1/2" thick. This is the base of the pot. Place it on the cardboard square.

3. Roll a chunk of clay into rope-like thickness to a length that will fit around the clay base. Roll the clay out on the waxpaper from the middle to the ends using both hands.

4. Dip fingers into the water. Run the water around the edge of the clay base and/or score/scratch with a toothpick. Coil the clay rope on the inside of the edge. Press the ends together.

5. Roll out a second rope of clay. Run water over the top of the first coil and form a second coil. Make sure that the coils do not connect on the same side. The completed pot is about 2" high and 3" in diameter.

6. Use a toothpick to engrave designs on the coils or smooth out the coils using the stone or plastic egg half on the inside of the pot and patting and smoothing the coils on the outside with the wooden spoon. Be sure the coils are bonded together on the inside and outside of the pot before it is fired.

Slipping and Polishing a Small Pot

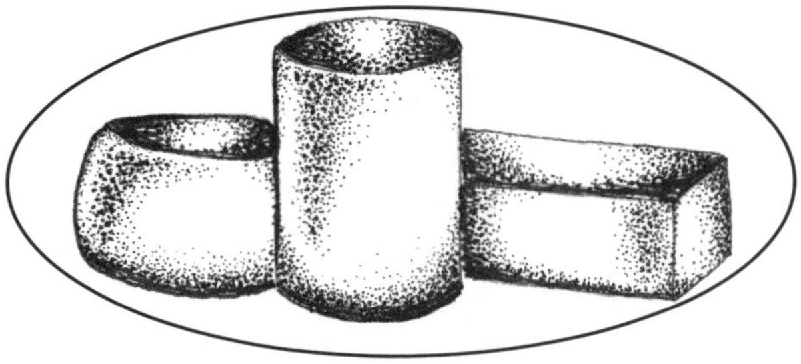

Materials

Clay pot - Use the coiled pot made from the previous activity. Be sure it is completely dry, but not fired.
***AARDVAK®* gray or red clay cone .06 -** for slip
Sandpaper - fine grain sandpaper
Small bowl - Cover just he bottom with water.

Polishing Stones - smooth river stone, large marble, or tumbled stone
Cloth - small square of soft cloth (old T-shirt)

This pot may be taken to a ceramic shop and fired in a kiln at cone .06. The slip must be completely dry before firing.

1. Use sandpaper to smooth and rub out rough lumpy surface of dried pot. Be gentle, do not rub too hard.

2. Make a slip from a different colored clay than that of the completed pot. Mix clay with water to the consistency of melted ice cream.

3. Dip cloth into the slip and spread it on a small area on the bottom of the pot.

4. Gently rub the polishing stone in circular or back and forth motions over the slipped area.

5. Continue to slip small sections of the pot and polish. Pour some of the slip inside. Tip the pot so the inside is covered with the slip. Polishing is not necessary on the inside, but can be done if desired.

6. In place of the slip, water may be used. Dip the cloth in the water and spread it over the small area on the pot. Polish this area with a smooth stone.

Clay Figurines

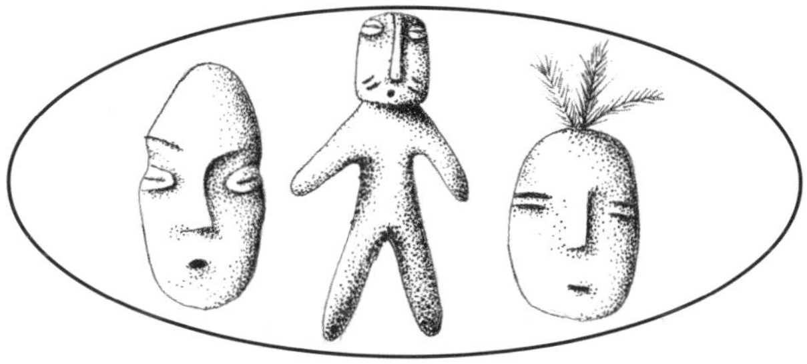

Materials

***AARDVARK®* gray clay cone .06**
(Other types of clay may also be used.)
Sandwich bag – Place an 8 oz. piece of clay in the bag. Close the bag after each removal of clay.
Wax paper – cut a 12" x 14" square

Masking tape – Tape the wax paper square to a flat surface. Run the tape completely across the top and the bottom of the square
Toothpicks
Feathers

The figurine may be taken to a ceramic shop and fired in a kiln at cone .06. Allow it to dry about a week before firing.

1. Roll a chunk of clay into a rope-like thickness.

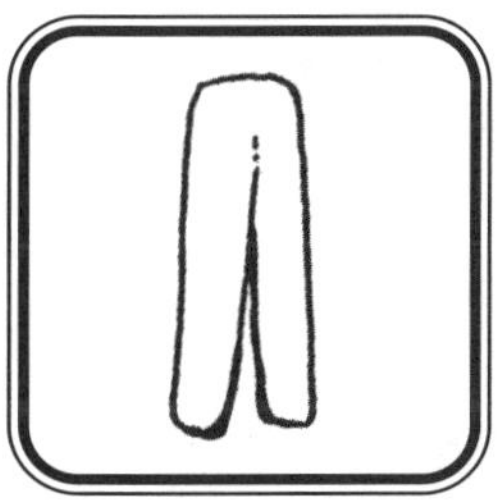

2. Fold the rope of clay in half or use two rolls pinched together at the top.

3. Where the rope bends, shape it into a head or flatten the place where the rope bends and add a piece of clay for the head. Before adding a piece of clay for the head, score (incise) it with a toothpick. Pinch out the nose and ears. Smooth the clay where the torso is.

4. Roll out a second rope of clay for the arms. Pinch off the ends at a suitable length. Before placing the arms on the back, score (incise) it with a toothpick.

5. Place the rope of clay over the scored clay and press pieces together. The arms may then be moved in the desired position.

6. Use a toothpick to add eyes, mouth, hair, and clothing features. Feathers may be stuck into the head as a headdress. (Be sure to remove them before firing, and replace them after with a little glue.)

Hohokam Shell Jewelry

The Hohokam obtained shells through trade or by making trips on foot to the Gulf of California The Hohokam may be thought of as the trend setters in the development of shell jewelry. They were making it long before their Mogollon and Anasazi neighbors, and were, in fact, responsible for trading ornaments of shell to them.

Shell bracelets were the most common ornament made. They were manufactured from a whole *Glycymeris gigantea* shell (commonly called bittersweet clam). Stone tools were used to make these bracelets. The shell was rubbed on a piece of gritty stone to wear a hole in the center. A small hammerstone was then used to break out more of the center of the shell. A stone reamer was used to grind out the opening and further enlarge and smooth it. This process continued until just the outer ring of the shell remained. The Hohokam sometimes carved geometric designs or animal shapes on these shell bands.

Necklaces were made by stringing whole shells or flat disc beads manufactured from the shell. The spire end (the tapered point of a spiral shell) of *Olivella dama* shells (commonly called olive shells) were ground away making an opening so that they could be strung. Disc beads were shaped from cut squares of shell. Next a hole was drilled in the center of these shell blanks. They were then strung and rolled back and forth on abrasive stone to smooth and shape them into round flat beads for necklaces and anklets. Earrings and pendants were sometimes made of whole shells or shells carved into different life forms. Some pendants were etched, painted, or decorated with mosaic overlay. The Hohokam used turquoise and shell chips in their mosaic overlays. Archaeological evidence shows that lac was used as an adhesive. Lac is a resinous substance manufactured by the lac insect from the juices of the creosote bush. The turquoise chips were usually rectangular or triangular, in shape, but round, curved irregular or complicated geometric shapes were also used. The turquoise and shell chips were laid on top of the lac-coated shell, thereby the name of mosaic overlay instead of inlay. Two common mosaic shapes were the frog and the bird. Sometimes whole *Glycymeris* shells were encrusted with turquoise mosaics.

The Hohokam also etched designs in shell. They were etching shell hundreds of years before the Renaissance armorers in Europe came upon the technique. It is thought that the Hohokam used a weak acetic acid made from fermented juice of the saguaro fruit to etch the shell. A resistant substance, such as a pitch from the mesquite or the lac from the creosote was used to coat a design or place around a design on the shell. The *Laevicardium elatum* shell (commonly called the giant egg cockle) was preferred for etching. When the shell was placed in the vinegar-like fruit juice, the unprotected shell surface was eaten away. When the desired depth of etching had been reached, it was removed from the solution, and the pitch scraped away revealing a raised design. Etching occurred on both the inside and outside of the shell and sometimes on both. Occasionally the raised design was painted.

Glycymeris gigantea - The largest of the two Glycymeris species is commonly called bittersweet clam. It has rust-brown spots that give a zigzag effect.

Hammerstone - A stone held in the hand and used as a hammer.

Olivella dama - A small Olivella shell no larger than 3/4".

Lac - A sticky resinous substance not soluble, manufactured by the female lac insect, *Tachardiella larrea,* from the juices in the creosote bush. The lac is secreted from the insect's glands onto the branches of the bush. These encrustations or "scale" are scraped from the bush. When heated, it softens to a plastic state and can be used as a bonding material. When it cools, it is impenetrable.

Acetic - Pertaining to or like vinegar.

Etching Shell

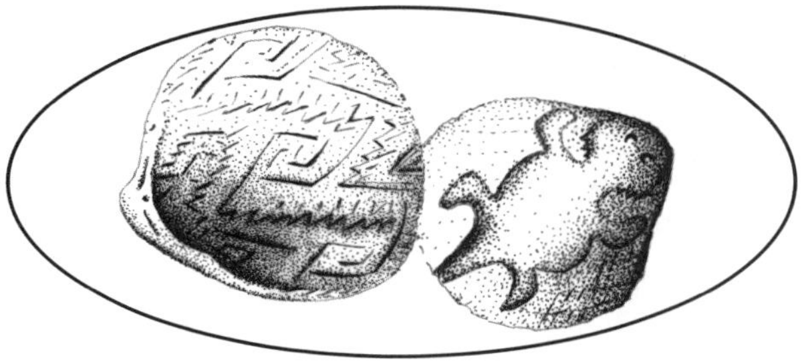

Materials

Shells – with smooth surfaces
(The insides of shells may also be used.)
Vinegar
Soapy water
Acetone or nail polish remover
Paper towels

Pencil
Dark colored nail polish
Plastic cup
Toothbrush
Clear nail polish – place over penciled name or initials if more than one person's shell is being etched.

1. Draw a design with a pencil on the smooth surface of the shell.

2. Brush colored nail polish on the whole drawing for a positive design or around the drawing for a negative design.

3. When the nail polish is dry, place the shell in a plastic cup. Cover the shell with vinegar. Leave the shell in the vinegar over night or longer until the desired depth of etching is reached. (Watch closely so that the shell does not get "eaten" through.)

4. Remove the shell from the vinegar when the desired depth of etching is reached. Rinse the shell in soapy water to remove the effects of the vinegar.

5. Take a paper towel or a rag dipped in nail polish remover or acetone and rub off the nail polish.

6. Dip an old toothbrush in acetone and scrub out the nail polish remaining in the grooves of the shell. Rinse the shell in soapy water.

Shell Bead Necklace

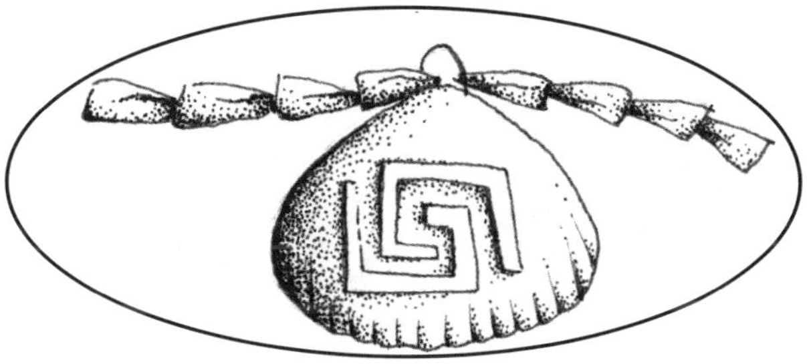

Materials

Sandstone – rough stone or sandpaper
Small shells – shells with spires (the tapered point of a spiral shell)
Candle
Large shell – Use the etched shell from the previous activity, or a large smooth shell about 1" to 2" in diameter.

Acrylic paints
Brush
Pencil
Wire or hairpin
Hot glue gun and glue sticks
Crochet thread - 100% cotton – measure to fit over the head

1. Sand down the spire end of the small shell until a hole is worn through.

2. Using a pencil, draw a design on the large shell. Choose a design from the pages in the back of this book or create a design.

3. Paint over the penciled design with acrylic paints. If an etched shell has been completed, the raised design may be painted.

4. Dip the end of the necklace thread in melted wax from a candle or in clear nail polish. (Adults should help with this activity.)

5. Using a hot glue gun, place a small amount of glue on the inside at the top of the rim of the shell. Place a wire loop or hairpin in the glue. (Adults should help with this activity.)

6. String half of the small shells first, then the large shell and then the rest of the small shells. Knot the ends to complete the necklace.

Mosaic Shell Pendant

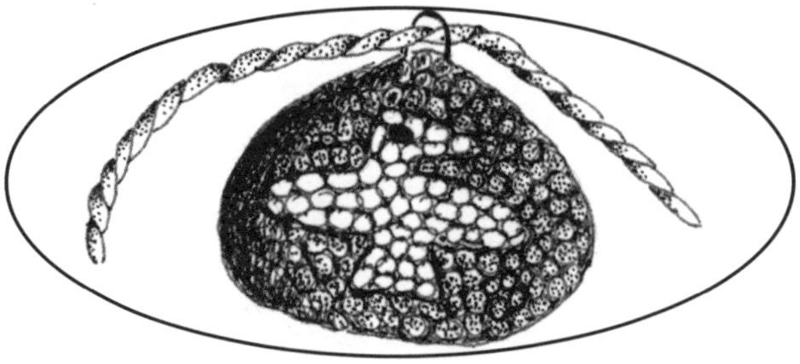

Materials

Shell – with smooth surface
Pencil
Fish tank gravel – 2 colors, blue and red
Permanent adhesive – a glue made for gluing rhinestones
Toothpicks – flat
Container or square of cardboard for adhesive
Wire or hairpin
Hot glue gun and glue sticks
Yarn or string - measured to fit over the head

1. Choose a simple design from the pages in the back of this book or create your own. Draw the design on the shell with a pencil.

2. Place the permanent adhesive in a small container or on a cardboard square.

3. Place a small amount of glue on a piece of gravel using a toothpick. Glue one color of the gravel pieces on the central parts of the design first.

4. Use the second color of the fish tank gravel to fill in around the design.

5. Using a hot glue gun, place a small amount of glue on the inside at the top of the rim of the shell. Place a wire loop or a hairpin in the glue. (Adults should help with this activity.)

6. Thread the yarn or string through the wire loop and knot it.

Hohokam Cotton Spinning

The Hohokam were among the first people to raise cotton in the United States Southwest. By hand, they dug canals that ran from the rivers to irrigate their fields of cotton, corn, beans, squash, and barley. How the Hohokam harvested, prepared, spun, and dyed their cotton is not known. What is known is based on limited archaeological evidence combined with knowledge about how cotton was raised by the historic Pima who live where the Hohokam once lived.

When the Spanish first met them in the late 1600s, the Akimel O'odham (Pima) were raising cotton as one of their crops. They used a stick to dig the holes for the seeds they planted. Like the Hohokam, they too, irrigated their crops through the use of canals. When the cotton bolls (pods) were mature, they were picked from the plant and spread on the roof tops to dry. Once dried, the cotton was pulled from the opened pods and stored in large pottery jars.

Before the cotton could be spun into yarn, it had to be ginned (the seeds removed) and carded (the fibers straightened). The Akimel O'odham women ginned and carded cotton as one of their household tasks. They first spread the cotton fibers out and then beat it with switches. This beating process sometimes accomplished both the ginning and carding.

The cotton was spun into yarn with the help of a spindle. The spindle consisted of a stick with a weight on it. The stick is the shaft of the spindle and the weight is the whorl of the spindle. The weight for the Hohokam spindle was a clay bead or a pot sherd disk. The Akimel O'odham used a crossbar spindle, which consisted of the stem of an arrow-weed plant as the shaft, (which was about 18" to 29" long) and a piece of saguaro rib (which was about 4" to 7" across) bound at a right angle across the arrow-weed stem (pluchea sericea) a few inches up from the bottom. The Akimel O'odham placed the crossbar spindle upright when spinning, resting the lower tip in a wooden cup or on the ground. The Hohokam may have used this same style of spindle but good evidence does not exist to confirm this. At many of the Hohokam village sites, archaeologists have found modeled clay beads and potsherd whorls (broken pieces of pottery that were shaped into a disk and then perforated). These whorls are all that remain of the Hohokam spindles. The shafts of the spindle could have been of bone or straight plant stalks.

Among the few woven products found at Hohokam sites, there is evidence of dyed yarns. Archaeologists found cotton yarns and textile remains when they excavated the Ventana Cave site. (This is a cave in the Castle Mountains of Southern Arizona, used by many people over the years, including the Hohokam.) Red is the most frequently dyed color of yarn. Other colors included brown and black. What was used as a dye is not known. The Akimel O'odham used an ocher (yellow or reddish brown earthy clay colored by an iron oxide mineral) to stain the edges (selvages) of their cotton cloth.

Cotton boll - The seed pod of the cotton plant.

Ollas - The Spanish word for the wide mouthed jars usually made of clay.

Ginned cotton - The cotton fibers that have had the seeds removed.

Carded cotton - The cotton fibers that have been straightened.

Spindle - The spindle is a hand tool used to spin cotton fiber into yarn. It consists of a stick, the shaft, and a weight, which is the whorl.

Selvage - A specially woven edge that prevents cloth from raveling.

Spindles

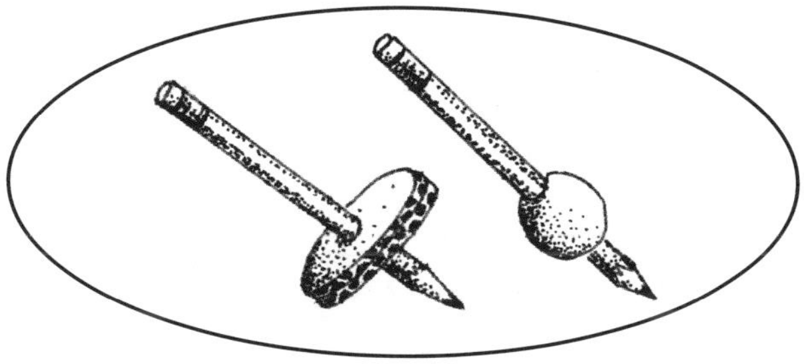

Materials

Materials for a cardboard whorl

Cardboard – corrugated grocery carton
Glass – juice glass with a rim that measures about 2 1/4" in diameter to be used for tracing cardboard circles
Glue – white glue
Pencil – new, sharpened pencil
Scissors

Materials for a clay whorl

Pencil – new, sharpened pencil
Clay – plasticine clay – an oil base clay that does not dry hard

DIRECTIONS FOR TWO DIFFERENT WHORLS

CARDBOARD WHORL

1. Trace two circles using a juice glass rim or other circular object on the cardboard. Cut out the circles.

2. Spread glue on one cardboard circle. Place the second circle on top. Press the two circles together.

3. Find the center of the cardboard circle. Puncture the disk with the point of the pencil. Push the disk up from the point about 1 3/4".

CLAY WHORL

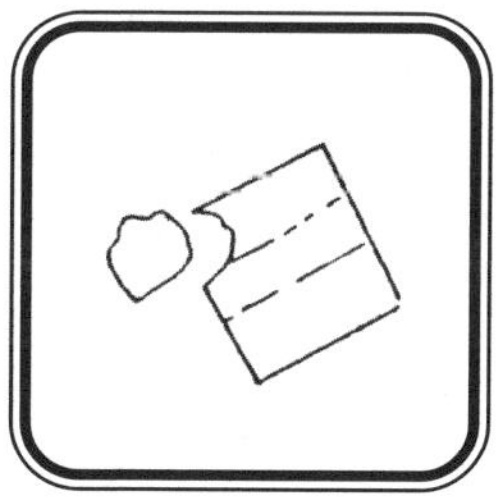

1. Pinch off a piece of the plasticine clay about the size of a walnut.

2. Roll the plasticine clay into a rounded ball.

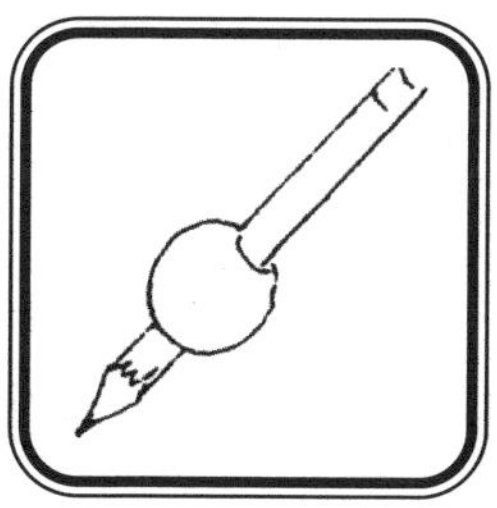

3. Pierce the center of the clay ball with the point of the pencil. Push the clay up from the point 1 1/2".

Spinning With Cotton

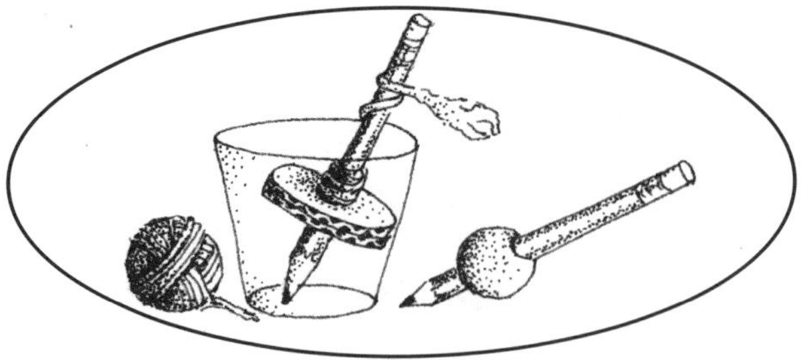

Materials

Spindle – Use the spindle made in the previous activity.
Cup – 9 oz. clear plastic solo cup or a custard cup

String – cotton string or yarn – cut into a 12" length
Cotton – cotton cosmetic putts, 100% cotton or acrylic

1. Take the end of the 12" string or yarn and tie it around the pencil right below the whorl. Bring the string up over the whorl and twist it around the pencil (clockwise if right-handed, counter clockwise if left-handed or which ever feels comfortable).

2. Straighten out the fibers of the cotton puff. Pull and fluff the fibers to about a 9" length. Give this length of fibers a slight twist.

3. Take the end of the string and place about an inch of it on top of the cotton. Fold the cotton over the string.

4. Hold the connecting spot of cotton and string. Spin the pencil clockwise with the right-hand or counter clockwise with the left-hand. Spin the pencil until the leader string is twisted tightly within the cotton.

5. Place the spindle in the cup, with the sharpened tip down. Hold the spun connection and pull a short tail from the cotton length. Again spin the pencil to twist the cotton fibers around each other creating a cotton yarn.

6. Stop spinning, and hold the place where the spun yarn ends. Pull out another short section of cotton fibers and spin the pencil. Continue spinning until all of the cotton fibers are spun. As the yarn is spun, it may be twisted around the pencil above the whorl.

Dyeing Cotton Yarn

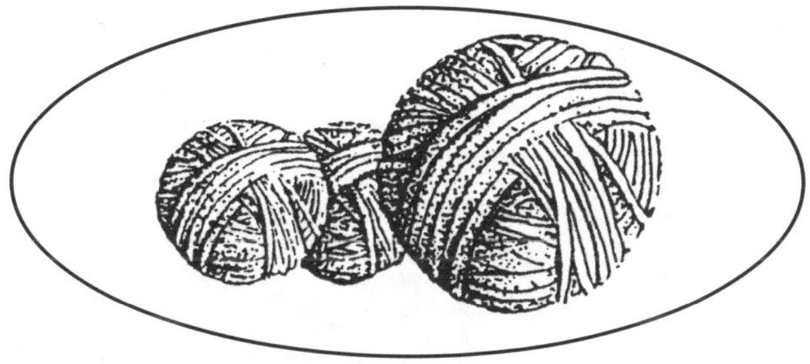

Materials

Cotton yarn – Use the cotton yarn on the spindle from the previous activity.
Kool-Aid® – 2 packets, unsweetened *Kool-Aid®*
Ceramic Cup – a coffee cup is fine
Boiling water – enough to fill the cup

Spoon
Plastic spool – empty plastic thread spool
Paper towels
Cardboard – Cut cardboard into a 4" by 3" square. Cut a slit at two diagonal corners.

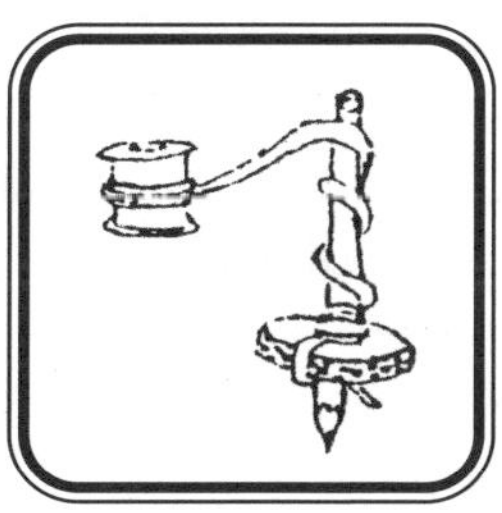

1. Remove the cotton yarn from the spindle and wind it onto a plastic thread spool

2. Pour *Kool-Aid®* from a packet into a cup. Two packets may be used for a deeper color.

3. Fill the cup 3/4 full of boiling water. Stir the mixture with a spoon to help the *Kool-Aid®* dissolve.

4. Place the spool with the cotton yarn into the hot *Kool-Aid®*. Place the spoon on top of the spool to hold it down. Leave it in the *Kool-Aid®* for 20 minutes or until the yarn is the desired color.

5. Remove the spool from the *Kool-Aid®* with a spoon. Pat the excess liquid from the yarn with a paper towel.

6. Place loose yarn end through the slit at one corner of the cardboard. Wind the damp yarn from the spool onto the cardboard. Leave space between each wrap. Place the opposite end through the other corner slit. Let it dry. This yarn can then be used in the weaving activity.

Hohokam Cloth Weaving

Redrawn from 1854 sketch in Bartlett's *Personal Narrative of Explorations and Incidents.*

Some archaeologists think that the Hohokam were the first southwesterners to use cotton in their textile art. They then introduced cotton to their neighbors to the north and east, the Anasazi and the Mogollon, through trade.

The Hohokam wove cotton cloth for blankets, breechcloths, belts, and ponchos. Their textile remains do not preserve well, because their houses were built in the open and they practiced cremation as part of their funeral rites. Some textile remains were preserved because they were carbonized in cremation fires and did not burn completely. Other textile remains that did survive are from dry cave sites. Hohokam cotton cloth is a dull white and of a plain weave with some weft-wrap openwork. (Weft-wrap openwork is cloth with small holes created during weaving. The holes are so placed in the cloth to form a pattern.)

Textiles found in Ventana Cave (a cave site with Hohokam perishable artifacts), and Snaketown, (a Hohokam village site south of Phoenix), were plain, gauze, and weft-wrap open work weaves. The Hohokam dyed the warps and wefts of the plain weave different colors to give them patterns.

The yarns that run vertical on a loom are the warps. The yarns that pass over and under the warps horizontally are the weft yarns. It is only assumed that the Hohokam loom was a heddle-equipped, horizontal loom. A Heddle is a rod strung with string loops that encircle one set of warps. When it is raised up, the warps attached separate away from a second set of warps creating a shed or opening for the weft thread to pass through and complete a row of weaving. Although there is not any recognizable archaeological remains of Hohokam looms in southern Arizona, there is historic evidence of the use of a horizontal loom by the Tohono O'odham (Papago), Akimel O'odham (Pima), and Maricopa (Xalychidom Piipaaash).

The Akimel O'odham began building a horizontal loom by driving four stakes in the ground. These stakes outlined the rectangular size of the cloth to be woven. River sand was spread on the ground to keep the underside of the woven cloth clean. They then lashed saguaro ribs to the end stakes with cord. It was over and under these ribs that the warp yarn passed. A buff colored binding thread was looped around the ends of the warp yarns and tied to the saguaro ribs. When the weaving became too far away to reach, the weaver moved up and sat upon the weaving and continued. The weft thread was tied to the end of an arrow-weed stick for a shuttle. When the heddle was raised, the shuttle was passed through the opened shed. A batten made from mesquite wood was used to beat down the weaving. They also used a batten to keep the shed open to pass through the shuttle.

In John R. Bartlett's *Personal Narrative of Explorations and Incidents* which was published in 1854, there is a sketch of a horizontal loom and someone busy weaving. He states that, "The warp is attached to two sticks, and stretched upon the ground by means of stakes. Each alternate thread of the warp is passed round a piece of cane, which being lifted, opens a passage for the shuttle in the manner of a sley."

Note - The sketch at the beginning of this segment is an enhancement of the drawing found in Bartlett's personal narrative showing a horizontal loom being used in a Pima village.

Textile - Any material that is woven.

Breechcloth - A cloth worn about the buttocks.

Poncho - A blanket like cloak with a hole in the center to put on over the head.

Cremation - The burning of a dead body.

Warps - The yarns placed lengthwise or that run vertical on the weaving loom.

Wefts - The yarns that pass horizontally over and under the warps.

Heddle - Is a rod strung with string loops that encircle one set of warps.

Shuttle - A device, such as a stick, wound with the weft yarn which is passed through the shed from one side of the loom to the other.

Batten - Usually a light strip of wood inserted between the two sets of warps that then opens the shed for the shuttle to pass through.

Sley - From Bartlett's description of a sley, it acts as a heddle on a weaving loom.

Warping a Loom

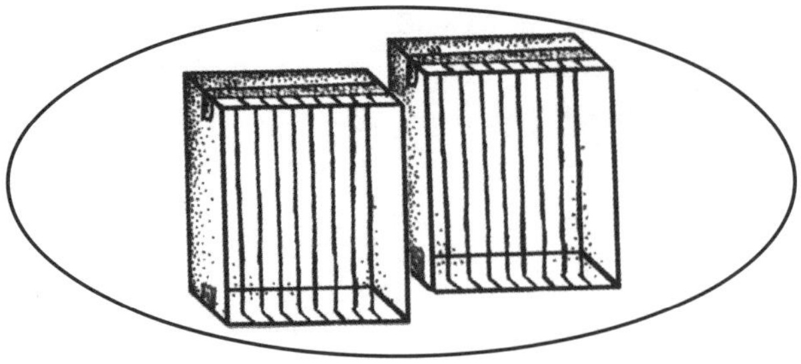

Materials

String - to warp the loom use 14' for 8 to 10 warps; use 17' for 12 to 14 warps
Masking tape
Cardboard tray - cardboard beverage tray or box lid 11" by 16" and about 2" deep

Ruler
Scissors
Pencil

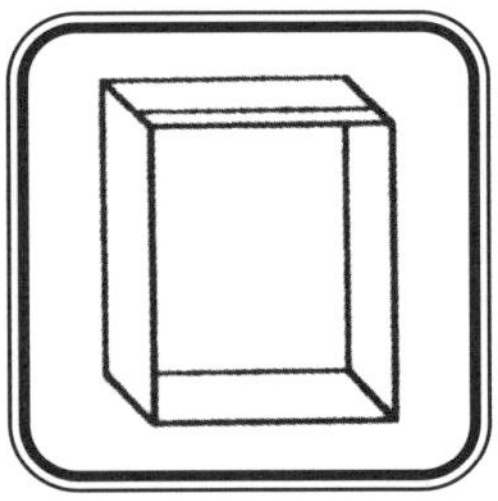

1. Measure and draw a line 3/4" from the edge on both short ends of the cardboard lid or beverage tray.

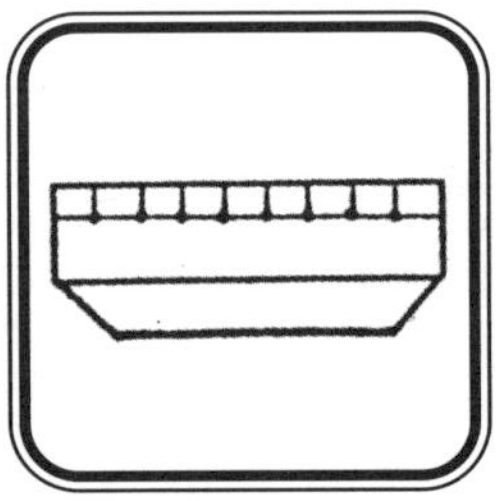

2. Make dots at ever 1/2" on the drawn lines. Cut a slit from edge to dot. Cut only 8 to 10 slits in the center for younger children and 12 to 14 in the center for older children.

3. Tie a knot at the end of the string. Slide the string through the designated first slit at the top of the tray so the knot is on the outside of the box. (Placing the string on the loom is called warping.)

4. Bring the warp string from the top slit to the opposite bottom slit. Slide the string through the slit. Now bring the string through the slit next to it and up to the top slit opposite it. Repeat until you have the correct number of warp threads.

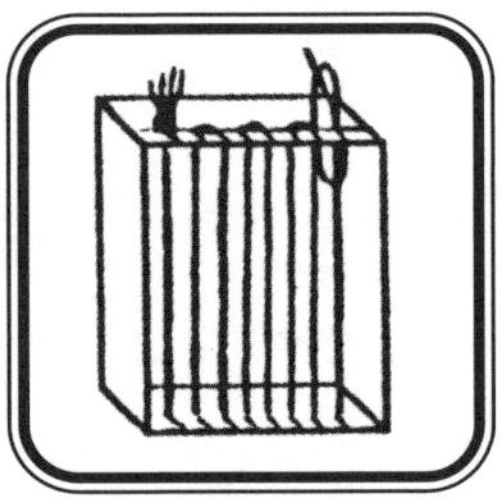

5. Be sure the warp strings are tightly stretched. To secure the string at the end, loop it around and between the last two slits and tie a knot.

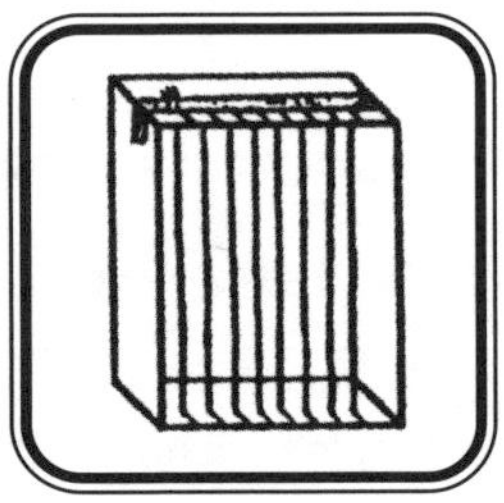

6. Place a strip of masking tape over each end of the box, covering the warp stitches to keep them from pulling out of the slits.

Plain Weaving

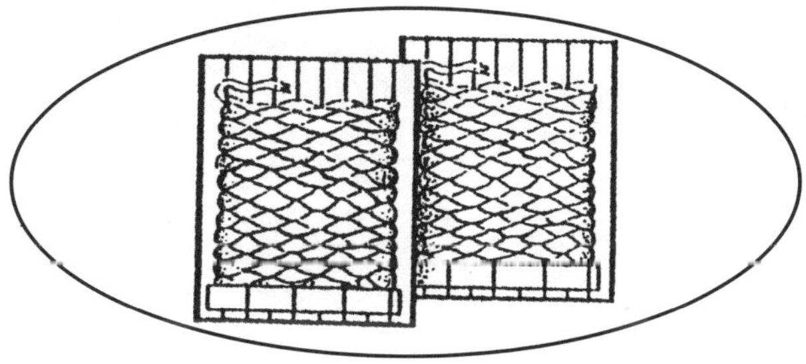

Materials

Box lid loom - Use the warped loom made from the previous activity.
Yarn - Rug yarn (*Aunt Lydia's®* or other heavy craft yarn is best for beginners.) Cut the yarn into one yard lengths.
Cardboard - Cut into 3" by 9" for the loom
Scissors
For added fun - weave with different textured yarns, strips of cloth, sisal, or other strips of material

Suggestion: Do not pull the weft yarns too tightly - otherwise the finished weaving will have an hourglass shape.

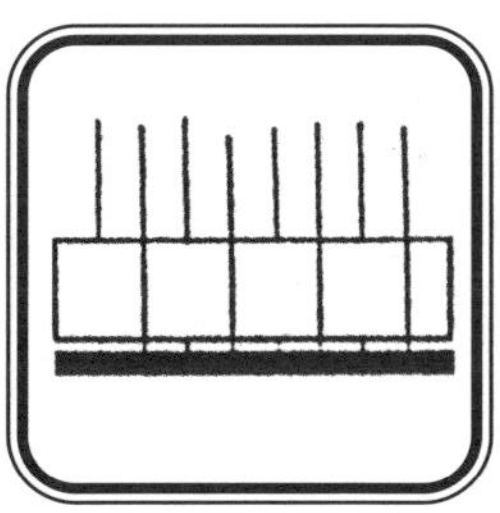

1. Weave a cardboard strip across the bottom of the warped loom. The bottom is the end opposite the warped beginning.

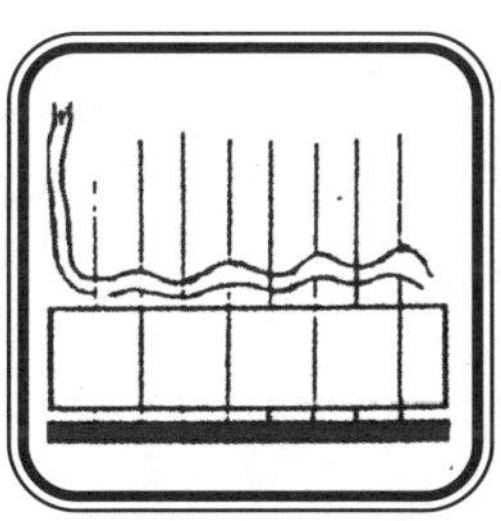

2. Begin to weave on the left side with one 36" length of yarn. Place the yarn over or under the first warp. Weave the yarn (weft) over and under all of the warps and then pull the rest of the yarn length through leaving a tail end of about 6".

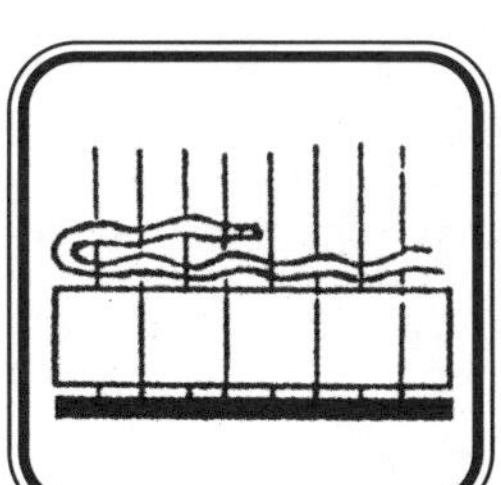

3. Weave the tail back to the center. Leave an end of about 2" tucked to the back side of the warps.

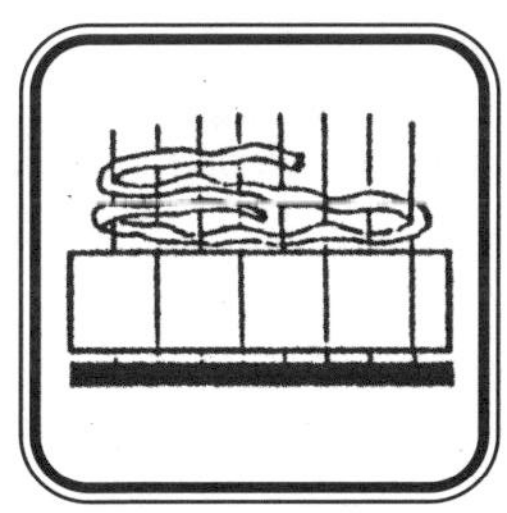

4. Take up the long end of the yarn and continue to weave. When coming to the end of this yarn, be sure the tail is tucked to the back of the weaving in the center of the warps.

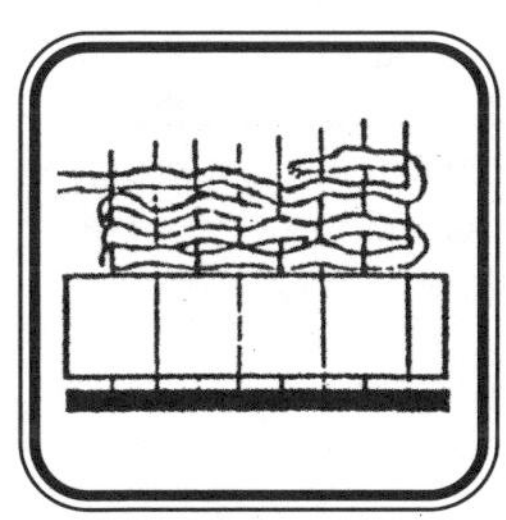

5. Begin a new yarn on the opposite side of the incomplete row of weaving. Begin in the way the first yarn was begun. Leave a tail and weave it back leaving 2" tucked to the back of the weaving.

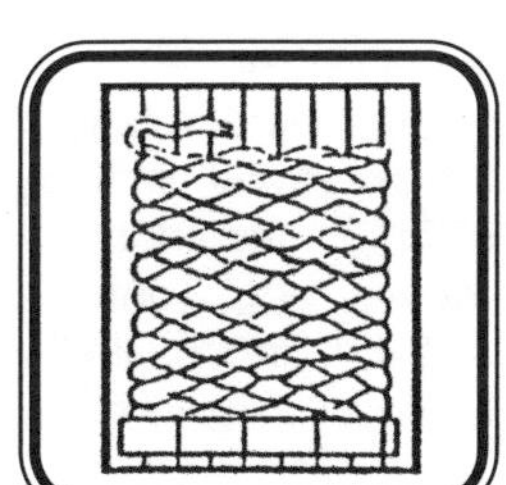

6. Continue to add new lengths of yarn until the weaving is about 4" from the top. The last 2" of yarn is tucked to the back of the waving. The weft yarns may be packed down so no warp strings show.

Removing the Weaving

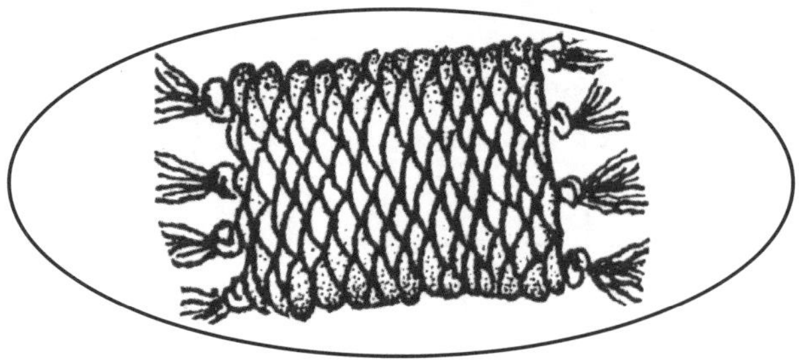

Materials

Finished weaving on box lid loom
Scissors

1. Cut two warp strings at the top of the loom. Cut the strings as close as possible to the box edge.

2. Pair the warp strings. Make a loop knot or half hitch with the pair. Tighten the knot right next to the weaving. Continue to cut two strings at a time and knot.

3. Remove the cardboard strip. Remove one warp loop at a time from the slits. Make a half hitch knot with the loop. Tighten the knot right next to the weaving. Continue to knot one loop at a time until all are knotted Then cut each loop.

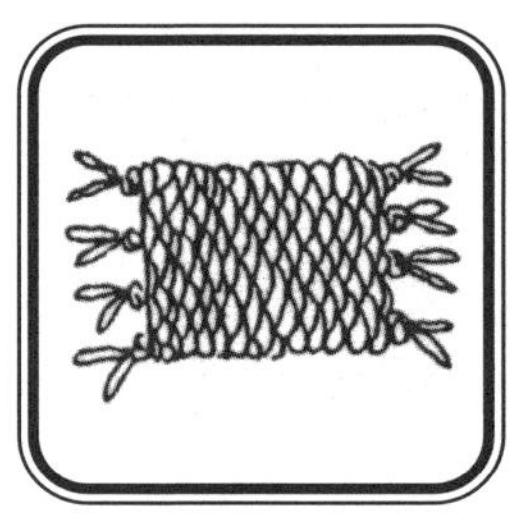

4. Cut the warp fringes to the desired length. Make the fringe on both sides even.

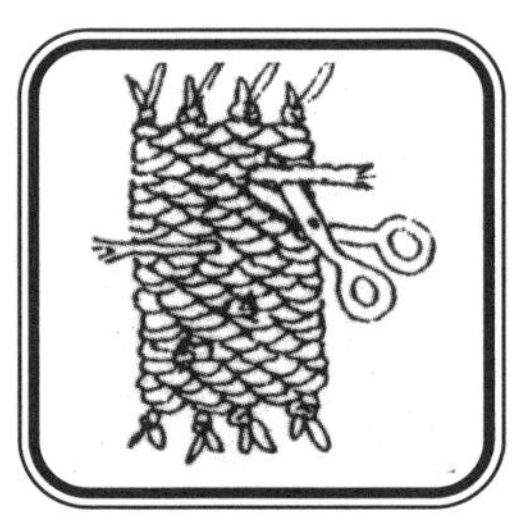

5. Turn the weaving over. Give a gentle tug to each yarn end. Cut the yarn ends off next to the weaving.

6. Unply or untwist each of the string fringe ends. Hold a string end in the air and pull apart its bundle of strands and let them untwist from around each other.

Hohokam Basket Weaving

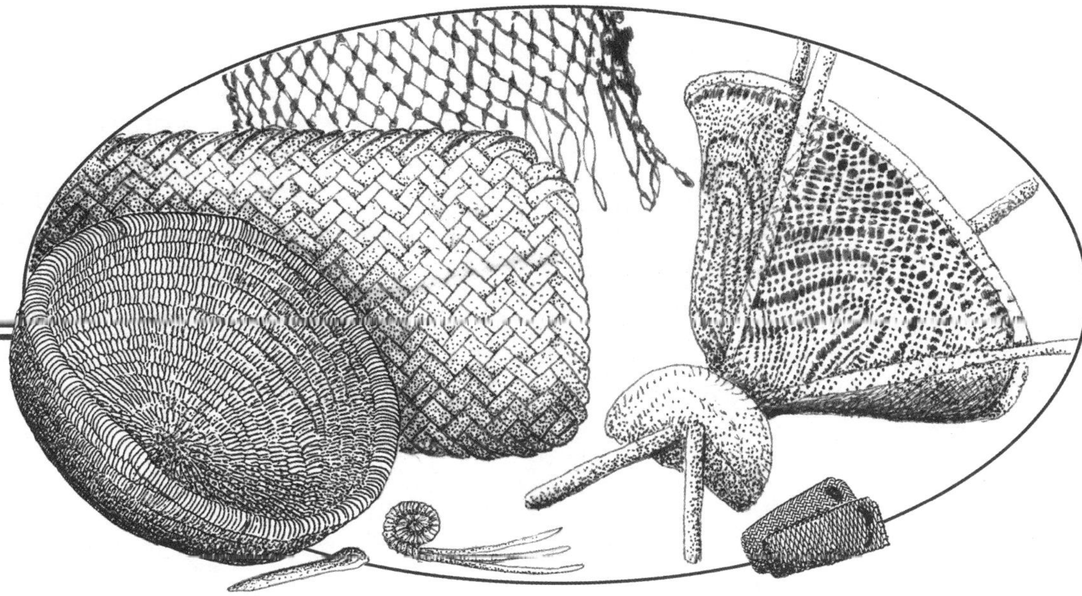

Archaeologists tell us that basketry is one of the oldest crafts. It predates pottery and loom weaving.

Over 10,000 years ago, the earliest people arrived in what is called today Arizona. These people followed the herds of animals they hunted. They would camp in an area for a season, or until they had completed a hunt or gathered seasonal plant food. When the game or plant food was no longer available, they moved. These hunters and gatherers were the first creators of basketry like containers. They needed to carry their hunted game or gathered plant foods and all their other possessions with them when they moved from camp site to camp site. Their earliest containers were probably net bags.

Net bags were not suitable for all burdens, so people created other styles. Burden baskets made with a netting placed over 4 rigid poles may have been one of the earlier styles of baskets. The Akimel O'odham (Pima) made a basket like this. It is called a *kiaha.*

Basket remains at many Hohokam sites are limited due to the location of their villages. They were built in the open desert and thus perishable items did not preserve well. The best preserved basketry comes from dry cave sites. Charred basketry fragments from cremations and impressions show that the Hohokam made coiled baskets and plaited mats. A coiled basket is very durable. It may be used to hold water, parch seeds, or carry heavy loads. Willow or cottonwood twigs were cut and split to obtain strips or splints of wood. These strips were wrapped around a foundation or core. The foundations of the Hohokam coiled baskets were one, two or three twigs or rods. Sometimes the rods included a bundle of shredded yucca leaves, cattail stem or finely split twigs. Once the woody strip was brought around the foundation, a hole was made in the finished coil below with a bone awl and the strip of wood poked through that hole and was pulled out the other side. Bone awls were also used as a punch for other purposes.

Plaited mat impressions have been found on the inner surface of clay jar stoppers, lumps of clay, side walls of houses, on the under surface of clay griddles called comales, and on house floors. These mat impressions show that river cane and leaf material such as yucca were used for plaiting. The impressions also showed patterns of plain plaiting and twill plaiting. Plain plaiting is the weaving of single strips of equal width and pliability over and under each other in a 1 over 1 pattern. This is known as a checker or plain weave. Twill plaiting is the weaving of pliable strips over and under two or more in the other set at staggered intervals. The twill plaiting has a pattern of 2 over 2, 3 over 3 or 4 over 4. It is sometimes known as diagonal plaiting, a chevron or her-ringbone weave.

From plaited mat impressions, archaeologists have learned that mats were slept upon, used as the side walls in their homes, to cook upon, and to use as a work surface when making their clay griddles. It was probably a good surface to manufacture the clay griddles for they could easily be removed from the mat when completed.

Charred - Something burned until it turns black.

Plaiting - A weaving technique in which there are two sets of flexible strips of material of the same width that cross over and under each other. If the pattern is over one under one, 1/1, it is a plain weave or checkered pattern. If the strips of material cross over or under more than one, it is called twilled plaiting.

Parch - To dry and slightly bake by exposing to extreme heat. Corn was parched by the Akimel O'odham (Pima) people by tossing the corn in a coiled basket tray with hot coals.

Splints - Thin, flexible strips of split wood used for basket making.

Awl - A pointed tool for making small holes. Bone was a common material used to make an awl.

Comales - Flat clay plates used as griddles for baking.

Plaiting a Mat

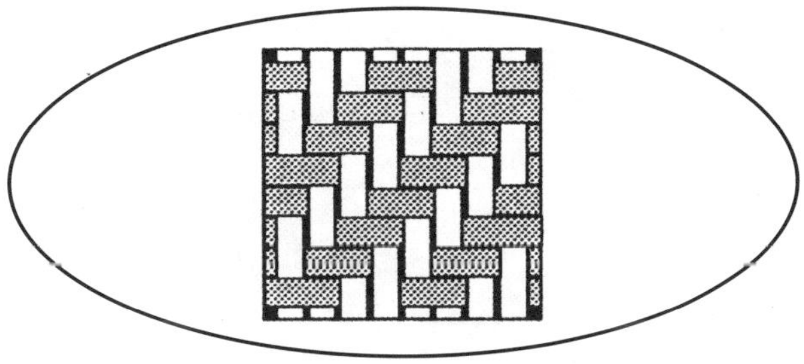

Materials

Black colored construction paper - cut 1 square measuring 6" by 6"
Scissors
Pencil
Ruler

Light - colored construction paper - cut 8 strips measuring 1/2" by 12" long
Contrasting colored construction paper - cut 8 strips measuring 1/2" by 12"
White glue

1. Draw a line down the center of the 6" square paper.

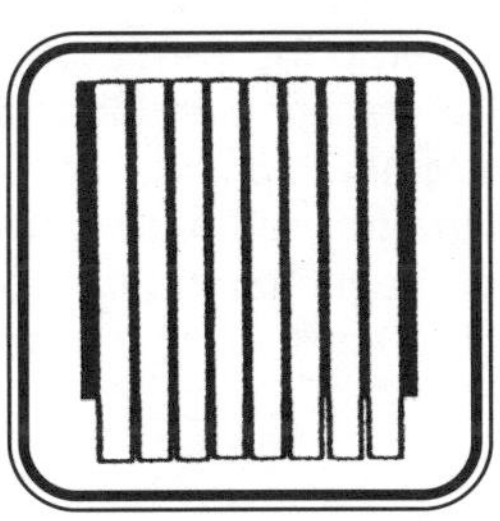

2. Place 4 of the light-colored strips on each side of the center line leaving a 1/2" edge on each side of the paper square.

3. Place glue 1/2" down on each strip of paper. Glue each strip to the top edge of the paper square.

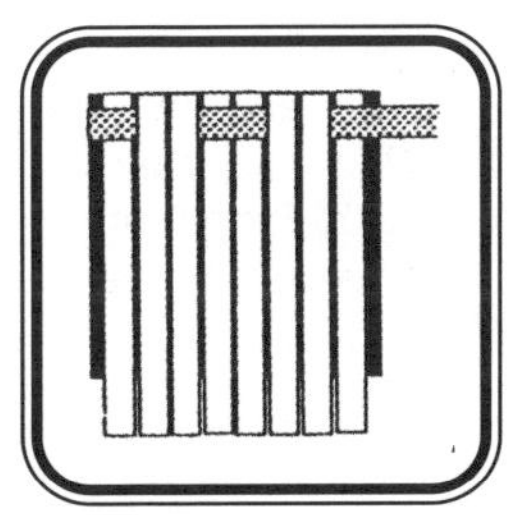

4. Take one of the contrasting strips of paper and begin to plait, over one under two, over two, under two, over one.

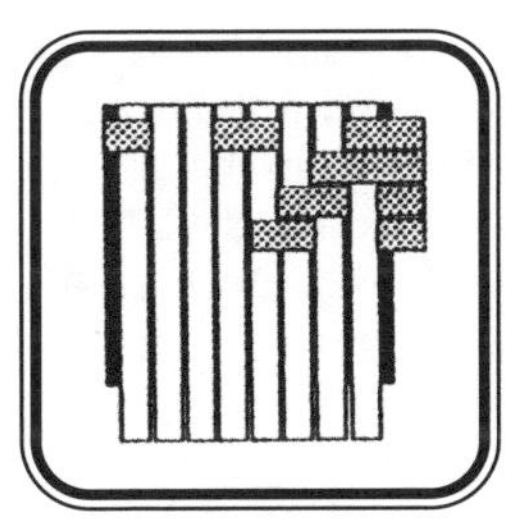

5. Take a second strip of paper and begin over two, under two, over two, under two. Begin the third strip under one, over two, under two, over two, under one. The fourth strip begins under two, over two, under two, over two. Repeat with the remaining 4 strips.

6. Glue the ends of each strip to the edges of the paper square. Cut the strips off that hang over the edge of the square. Many color combinations may be used for this project.

Coiling a Basket

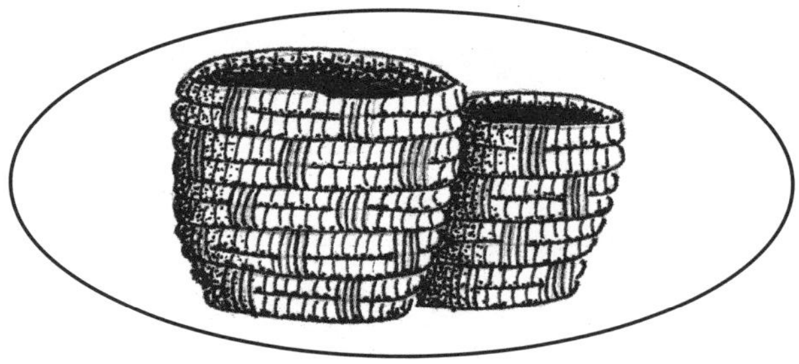

Materials

Cotton clothesline - sash cord, jute, upholstery cord, or nylon rope may also be used (These materials are used in place of plant material for convenience and conservation purposes.)
Rug yarn - 2 skeins, 3 ply *Aunt Lydia's®* yarn or other heavy yarn.

Plastic yarn needle - metal yarn needle or tapestry needle may be used
Scissors

1. Cut a 1 - yard length of rug yarn. Fold over end and thread the needle. To make the coiling move quickly, cut a 2 - yard length of rug yarn and double the yarn in the needle.

2. Unwrap the rope and leave it in a heap. Taper one end with the scissors. Begin to wrap the yarn end of the threaded needle 2" up from the tapered end. Over-lap the first wind to hold.

3. Bend the tapered end to meet the wrapped end. Wrap together to hold and form a loop. Then stick the needle through the center of the loop.

4. Wrap the yarn around the rope for 1/2". Bind this section to the beginning loop by wrapping the yarn around the rope and bringing the needle through the center. Repeat this 2 or 3 times. These are the coiling stitches. The first coil is bound to the beginning loop in this manner.

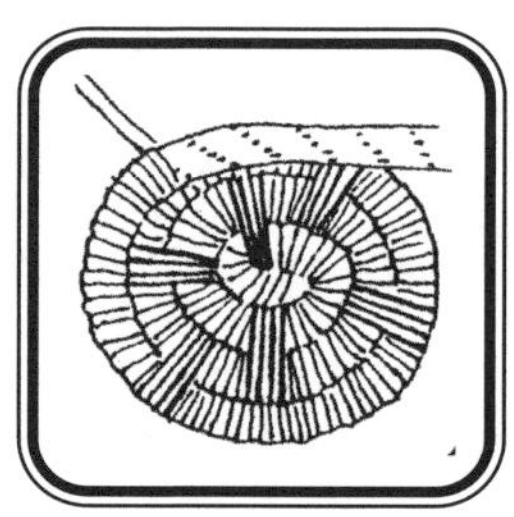

5. Continue to wrap the yarn around the rope in 1/2" sections and then bind to the coil underneath with two or three stitches until the desired base size is reached. Then begin to bind the coils on top of each other to form the basket sides.

6. TO ADD YARN run the needle back through the last 3 stitches and cut. Thread needle and run back out last 3 stitches and continue.
TO FINISH the last coil is ended where the first coil began. Bind the last inch of tapered cord to the previous coil.

Hohokam Gourds

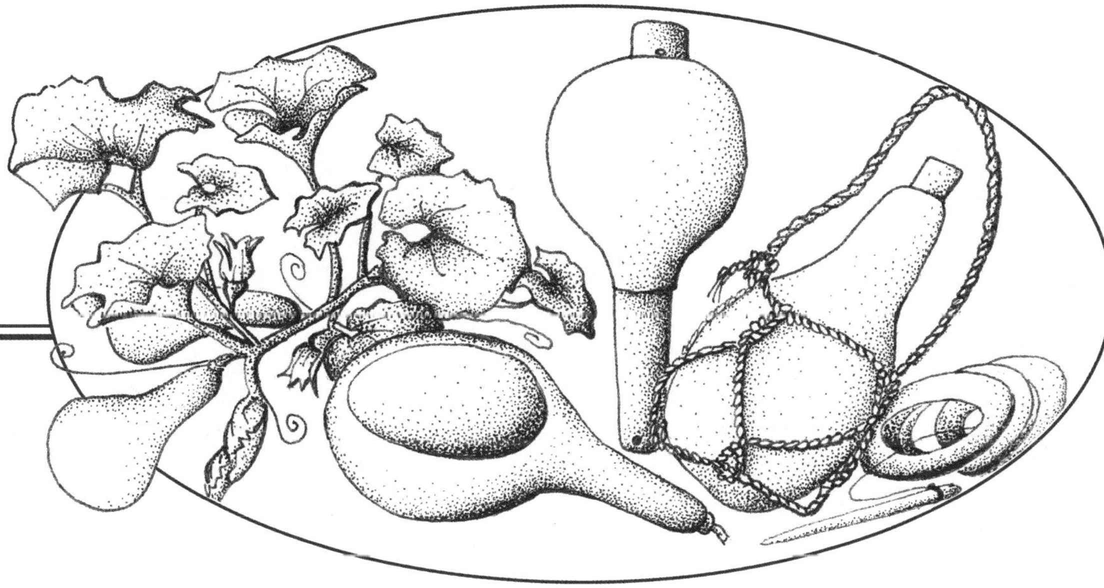

Long before pottery reached North America, gourds were being cultivated in the New World. Archaeologists uncovered bottle gourd *(Lagenaria siceraria)* fragments at Hohokam sites. These gourds have a long neck and look like a bottle. At one time these fragments could have been dippers, canteens, scoops, seed bottles, rattles, or game pieces. The Akimel O'odham (Pima), who today live along the Gila River where the Hohokam once lived, raised bottle gourds. Today, the chief use of the bottle gourd is for making rattles. It was reported in the early 1930's that seeds were not selected for specific shapes to propagate, but that farmers would wrap a piece of bark or cloth around the growing gourds to give them the desired shape.

In the past the Akimel O'odham planted their crops in hills. The gourd seeds were planted in early Spring when the mesquite trees began to leaf out. They were only planted when needed. Holes were dug with a stick about 2 to 3 inches deep. Four gourd seeds were placed in each and the dirt scraped over the hole with the foot forming the hill. They were planted near bushes or trees so that the plants could climb up the trunks. They were also planted near the irrigation ditches, because gourds required a lot of moisture. Sometimes during a dry season they would be watered by hand by the women. These plants were considered a woman's responsibility because they were thought to be an easy crop to grow. It would take a little more than 3 months for the gourds to ripen. They were then all gathered from the vines at once. A sharp stone was used to cut them from the vine. They were placed in a pile and covered with weeds or grass and left to dry. When dried completely, the stem end was cut and the gourd filled with water and let to stand until the fleshy interior would rot and decay.

Then a stick was used to remove the rotted pulp. This process was repeated until the gourd was cleaned. When the water in the vessel didn't taste bitter, it could be used for a canteen.

The Akimel O'odham used their gourds for canteens, dippers, containers, dishes, storage vessels, ceremonial rattles, and masks. If a gourd were to be used for a ceremonial rattle, the neck was cut off and pebbles taken from an ant hill and placed inside. A wooden handle was carved to fit into the opening and poke through the blossom end. It would be secured with the gummy secretion of the creosote. The Akimel O'odham medicine man or woman used the rattle in curing the sick or for ceremonies such as a girl's puberty dance or a dance for rain.

The Akimel O'odham also made a dart and ring game from gourds. The rings were cut from a gourd or squash rind. A soft squash was sliced crosswise into rings. The rings of various diameters were then pressed under something hard until flat and dried. As many as fourteen rings were strung on a fiber cord. Tied at one end was a piece of gourd larger than the opening of the smallest ring. At the other end was tied a pointed stick, the dart. The rings were tossed up into the air and the dart used to spear the rings. The Akimel O'odham kept score by moving beans or pebbles along a spiral decoration on a flat basket. This game may have been played by the Hohokam.

Bottle gourd - The *Lagenaria siceraria* is the gourd thought to have been cultivated 9000 years ago. It has a hard durable shell when dried. This bottle gourd has five basic shapes: dipper, bilobal, basket, trough, and snake.

Ramada - A shelter built of posts that support a roof that has open sides. A ramada provides shelter from the sun and the rain.

A Bag Rattle

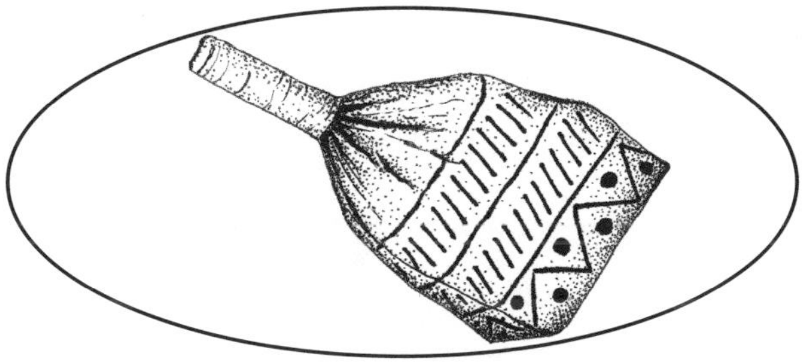

Materials

Heavy brown or white paper bag - The No. 2 size bag is preferred but the lunch bag size will do. (Bags are used in place of gourds for convenience.)
Masking tape - 1" wide

Scissors
Markers - crayons or paints may be used
Fine gravel - 8 dried beans, corn, or other hard seeds can also be used

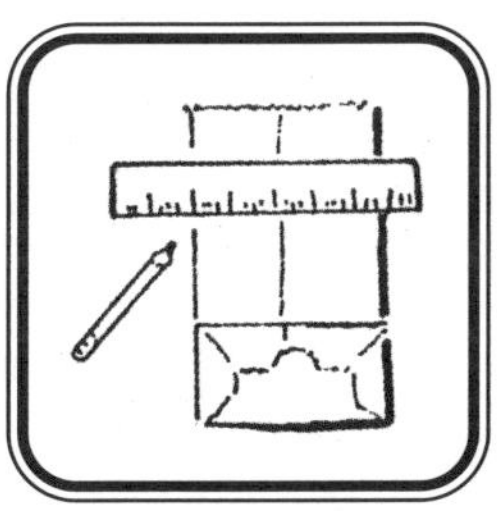

1. Draw a line 3" down from the top edge of the No. 2 bag or 4" down from the top edge of the lunch bag size. Draw the line on both sides of the bag.

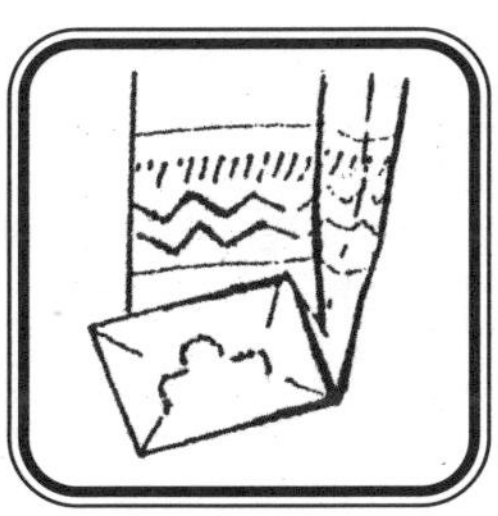

2. Use markers, crayons, or paints to make geometric designs below the line all around on the bag.

3. Open the decorated bag and place 8 dried beans, corn, other hard seeds, or fine gravel in the bag.

4. Blow up the decorated bag.

5. Crush the bag end into a handle above the design.

6. Wrap the masking tape around the squeezed end. cover the end completely. Now try the rattle for sound. (Try making different rhythms.)

Gourd Ring Toss Game

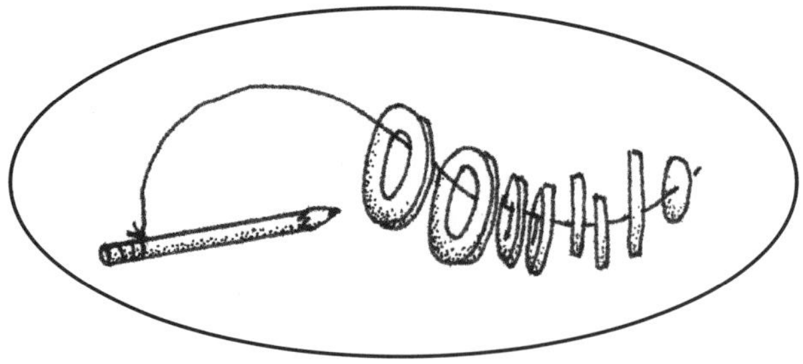

Materials

Plastic lids - 10 to 15 lids -- 2", 3", and 4" in diameter and any diameters in between. Obtain them from cheese, butter, frosting, syrup, etc. containers. (The plastic lids are used in place of gourds for convenience.)
Scissors - scissors with a sharp point such as cuticle or toenail scissors

Cardboard
Pencil - 6" to 8" long, sharpened
String - 18" in length
Ball point pen

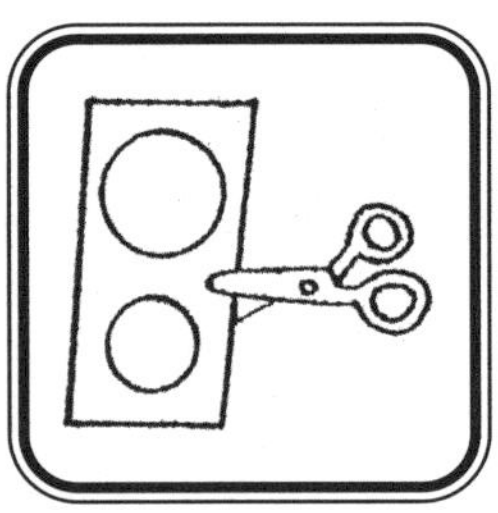

1. Cut two cardboard circles, one 2" in diameter and one 3" in diameter to use as patterns.

2. Trace around the 2" cardboard circle pattern in the center of all but one of the plastic lids, with a ball point pen.

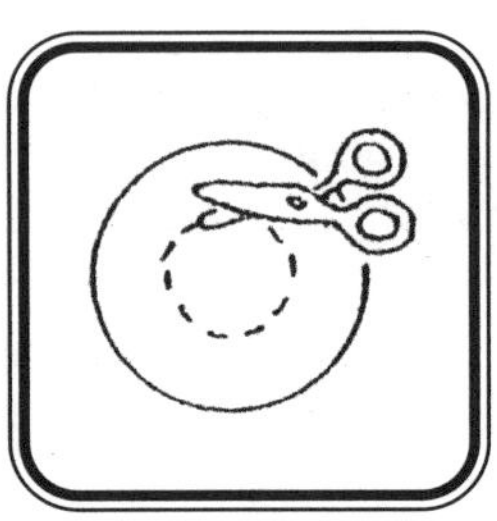

3. Use the cuticle or toenail scissors to cut out the circles traced on each of the lids. Be careful when punching the tip of the scissors through the plastic to begin cutting.

4. Tie the string at the eraser end of the pencil.

5. Cut around the 3" circle pattern on the spare lid. Cut out and then punch a hole in the center of the circle. Thread the string end through the hole and knot it.

6. Thread the pencil through the plastic rings, beginning with the smallest and ending with the largest. Hold the eraser end of the pencil, toss the string in the air and spear the rings with the pencil.

Hohokam Rock Art

Long before a written language was developed, people were carving and painting figures on rocks. These forms of expression are known today as rock art. Figures and designs carved, pecked, scratched, or engraved in stone are known as petroglyphs (*petro* meaning rock and *glyph* meaning carving). Painted figures are called pictographs, which are defined as "pictures representing ideas". Some of the earliest painted figures are found in caves in Europe, Africa, and Australia. The best known of these caves are Lascaux in France and Altamira in Spain. A more recent find in southeast France is Cosquer Cave. It was discovered in 1991 by Henri Cosquer a professional diver. Although the cave is half underwater, the walls above sea level are covered with engraved and painted figures. Carbon dating of the paint from the hand stencils has shown that they were done between 27,800 and 26,500 years ago.

The Hohokam primarily created petroglyphs. They used the direct percussion method. A sharp cobblestone, used like a hammer stone, was pounded directly on a rock surface. The rock faces and boulders that they usually chose were of some form of dark volcanic or other igneous rock. These rock forms take on a patination. This patina is the darkened surface of the rocks caused by a slow growing bacteria that oxidizes the minerals in the dust and cements them to the rock surface. (This process is still being researched.) As the dark rock surface is chipped away by the blows of the hammer stone, the lighter original color of the rock is revealed. The completed design stands out against the outer patinated rock surface.

Pictographs are found in the areas where the Hohokam lived, but it is not certain that they were made by the Hohokam. Along the wall of Ventana Cave (a cave site with Hohokam perishable artifacts) are painted a row of joined red triangles, like half of the border design found at the top of each page of this book. The red paint used to create these triangles was probably made from the mineral hematite.

The figures that the Hohokam chipped out on stone are either abstract or representational in style. They are scattered over rock surfaces in seemingly no particular order. The stick-like human figure is most frequent of the representational figures created by the Hohokam. This is sometimes known as a biomorph (a term used to denote figures that could either be human or animal). Some of the other representational figures are game animals such as deer, bighorn sheep, coyotes or dogs, birds, and lizards. Some of the abstract elements are spirals, mazes, frets, rectangular motifs, and circles. There are small single circles, concentric circles, circles joined by lines, circle clusters, and circles with dots. Spirals are seen throughout Hohokam rock art and are the hallmark of what is called the "Hohokam Gila Petroglyph style." Some of the Hohokam petroglyph designs are also found on their pottery.

What does it all mean? Because of the passage of time and today's cultural differences, Hohokam petroglyphs cannot be interpreted. But some rock art was made by people from Native American cultures still living today. Archaeologists have consulted with these people and looked at their cultural history and myths to help understand their rock art. Through this method, it has been learned that some petroglyphs and pictographs were created to ensure a good hunt, to tell a story, to mark a trail, or for ritualistic purposes.

Petroglyphs - Designs and figures carved, pecked, or engraved on stone.

Pictographs - Designs and figures painted on stone.

Percussion - The striking of one body against another such as a hammerstone pounded directly on a rock surface.

Cobblestone - A stone that is naturally rounded.

Patina - The darkened surface of the rocks caused by a slow growing bacteria that oxidizes the minerals in the dust and cements them to the rock surface.

Biomorph - A rock art figure that could either be human or animal.

Creating a Petroglyph

Materials

#150 grit sheet of sandpaper - cut the 9" by 11" sheet of sandpaper into four pieces each 4 1/2" by 5 1/2"
Newspaper
Large paper clip - straightened
Spray bottle - fill with water
Tubes of acrylic paint - red and brown
Tin can or plastic container
Paint brushes - 2 inexpensive 1 1/2" wide brushes
White glue - diluted with water in a cup
Mat board - cut 1" to 2" larger than sandpaper square

1. Squeeze a length of acrylic paint 2 1/2" long from tubes of brown and red into the container. Mix well with about 6 ozs. of water.

2. Place a sandpaper square on the newspaper. Coat the square with the reddish - brown paint. Let it sit for about 5 minutes or until the grit and glue coating on the sandpaper softens.

3. Test the sandpaper with a straightened paper clip in a corner. If the coating is soft enough, scratch out a petroglyph design with the paper clip.

4. Spray water on the sandpaper if it begins to dry and the glue hardens.

5. Spread the diluted white glue with one of the paint brushes on the back of the dry sandpaper petroglyph.

6. Place glued side of the sandpaper petroglyph on a piece of mat board 1" to 2" larger than the petroglyph art.

Notes

Notes

Notes

Snakes, Fish, and Scorpions

Tortoise, Lizards, and Horned Lizards

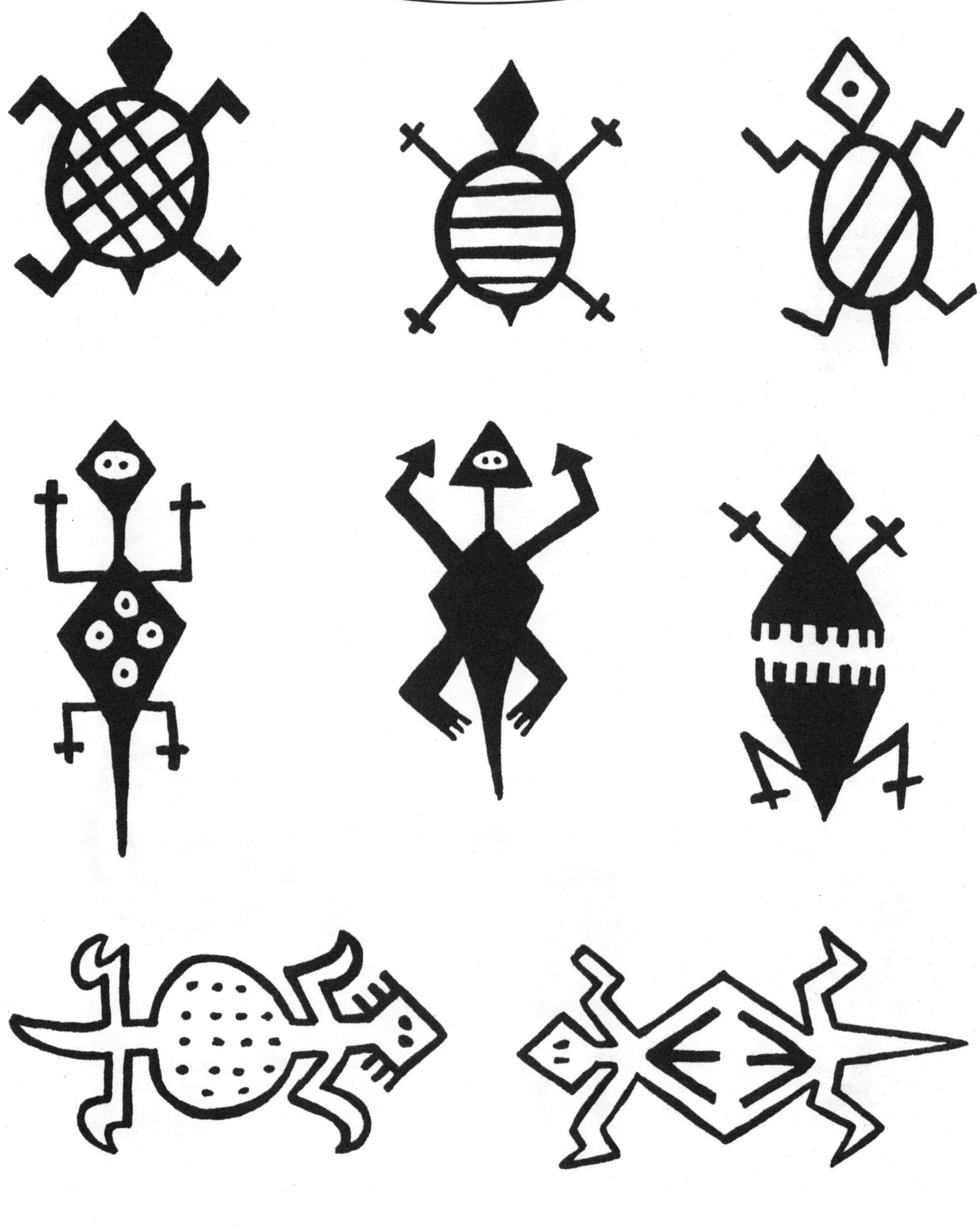

Human Figures

Birds

Mammals

Geometric Designs

Borders

References

Adovasio, J. M.
1977 *Basketry Technology: A Guide to Identification and Analysis.* Aldine, Chicago.

Bartlett, John Russell
1856 *Personal Narrative of Explorations and Incidents in Texas, New Mexico, California, Sonora, Chihuahua, etc.* New York.

Castetter, Edward F., and Willis H. Bell
1942 *Pima and Papago Indian Agriculture.* University of Arizona Press, Tucson.

Castetter, Edward F., and Ruth M. Underhill
1935 *The Ethnobiology of the Papago Indians.* University of New Mexico Bulletin No. 275. University of New Mexico, Albuquerque.

DiPeso, Charles C.
1951 *The Babocomari Village Site on the Babocomari River, Southeastern Arizona.* Amerind Foundation Papers No. 5. Amerind Foundation, Dragoon, Arizona.

Gladwin, Harold S., Emil W. Haury, E. B. Sayles, and Nora Gladwin
1965 *Excavations at Snaketown: Material Culture.* University of Arizona Press, Tucson.

Grant, Campbell
1967 *Rock Art of the American Indian.* Promontory Press, New York.

Gregonis, Linda M., and Karl J. Reinhard
1979 *Hohokam Indians of the Tucson Basin.* University of Arizona Press, Tucson.

Haury, Emil W.
1975 *The Stratigraphy and Archaeology of Ventana Cave.* University of Arizona Press, Tucson.

1976 *The Hohokam, Desert Farmers & Craftsmen: Excavations at Snaketown 1964-1965.* University of Arizona Press, Tucson.

Keen, Myra A.
1984 *Seashells of Tropical West America. 2nd edition.* Stanford University Press Stanford.

Kissell, Mary Lois
1972 *Basketry of the Papago and Pima Indians.* Rio Grande Press, Glorieta, N.M. (Originally published in 1916 by the American Museum of Natural History, New York.)

Masse, W. Bruce
1982 "Hohokam Ceramic Art: Regionalism and the Imprint of Societal Change." *Southwest Ceramics: A Comparative Review.* School of American Research Advanced Seminar, edited by Albert H. Schroeder. Arizona Archaeologist No 15. Arizona Archaeological Society, Phoenix.

Mielke, Judy
1993 *Native Plants for Southwestern Landscapes.* University of Texas Press, Austin.

Morris, Percy A.
1966 *A Field Guide to Pacific Coast Shells Including Shells of Hawaii and the Gulf of California.* 2nd edition. Peterson Field Guide Series. Houghton Mifflin., Boston.

Nabhan, Gary Paul
1985 *Gathering The Desert.* University of Arizona Press, Tucson.

Russell, Frank
1975 *The Pima Indians.* University of Arizona Press, Tucson. (Originally published as part of the Twenty-sixth Annual Report of the Bureau of American Ethnology, 1904-1905.)

Schaafsma, Polly
1980 *Indian Rock Art of the Southwest.* School of American Research, Santa Fe and University of New Mexico Press, Albuquerque.

Shepard, Anna O.
1976 *Ceramics for the Archaeologist.* Publication No. 609. Carnegie Institute of Washington, Washington, D.C.

Spier, Leslie
1978 *Yuman Tribes of the Gila River.* Dover Publications, New York. (Originally published in the United States in 1933.)

Underhill, Ruth
1941 *The Papago Indians of Arizona and Their Relatives the Pima.* United States Department of the Interior, Bureau of Indian Affairs, Washington, D.C.

CHILDREN'S READING LIST

Brandenberg, Aliki
1976 *Corn is Maize: The Gift of the Indians.* Harper Collins, New York.

Bret, Jan
1988 *The First Dog.* Harcourt Brace Jovanovich, San Diego.

Baylor, Byrd
1969 Before You Came This Way. Dutton, New York.

1972 *When Clay Sings.* Macmillan, New York.

1975 *The Desert Is Theirs.* Charles Scribner's Sons, New York.

1976 *And It is Still That Way.* Charles Scribner's Sons, New York.

1978 *The Way to Start a Day.* Charles Scribner's Sons, New York.

1981 *A God on Every Mountain Top.* Charles Scribner's Sons, New York.

Houk, Rose
1992 *Hohokam.* Southwest Parks and Monuments Association, Tucson.

Stokes, Michael, and William Lee Stokes
1980 *Messages On Stone.* Starstone, Salt Lake City, Utah.